1980

BOOKS BY EDWARD FIELD

Stand Up, Friend, With Me (Grove Press, 1963)

Variety Photoplays (Grove Press, 1967)

Eskimo Songs and Stories (Delacorte Press, 1973)

Sweet Gwendolyn and the Countess (Konglomerati Press, 1976)

A FULL HEART
by
EDWARD FIELD

Alma, you said I had a perfect love.
All I know is that my heart is full
and life has never been more beautiful.

The Sheep Meadow Press
New York City, 1977

Acknowledgments: Some of these poems originally appeared in *American Review, American Poetry Review, Cafe Solo, Harper's, Kenyon Review, Nausea, New Letters, The New York Review of Books, Poetry, Poetry Now,* and *Southern Poetry Review.*

Grateful acknowledgment is also made to the Creative Artists Public Service Program for their support.

Published by The Sheep Meadow Press
New York, New York

Cover design by Cathryn S. Aison
Printed and manufactured in the United States
by Faculty Press, Inc., Brooklyn, New York
Distributed by Horizon Press, 156 Fifth Avenue, New York 10010

ISBN 0-8180-1535-7 (cloth); 0-8180-1539-x (paper)
Library of Congress Catalog Card Number 76-57520
First printing

All my poems
are for you, dear one, first of all
(as my eyes are).

Then they are for my people everywhere.

Contents

Page

New York 1
Being Jewish 3
Roaches 6
Plant Poem 9
After the Moonwalk 10
A Visitation 13
The Drought 15
The Reservoir 19
To the Sikh Master, Kirpal Singh 21
The Impossibility of Finding a Guru 23
The Buddha, Radiant 24
The Teaching 26
Dying 28
Chopped Meat 30
Unwanted: A Villanelle 38
Diary: October 11, 1972 39
The Gods Desert Antony 41
The Lost, Dancing 42
The Book of Sorrow 43
Open Sesame 44
Ant 45
The Farewell 46
The Ghetto 47
Passover Meditation 48
Addressed to Angels, Not Humans 53
Both My Grandmothers 54
Nostalgie du Pays 57
In Memoriam 58
Beside a Pool 59
The Sand Map 60
The Celebrity 62
Football With the Sound Turned Off 64
The Two Orders of Love 66
David's Dream 68
Street Instructions: At the Crotch 70

Page

Wearing My Nose 72
In England 74
In the Can 77
Morning Song 79
Sonja Henie Sonnet 80
Pasternak: In Memoriam 81
Living With an Aries 83
Writing for Money 85
Longing for Lee Poe 86
Gone Blind 88
Visiting Home 90
Looking Back 102
Sharks 103

New York

I live in a beautiful place, a city
people claim to be astonished
when you say you live there.
They talk of junkies, muggings, dirt, and noise,
missing the point completely.

I tell them where they live it is hell,
a land of frozen people.
They never think of people.

Home, I am astonished by this environment
that is also a form of nature
like those paradises of trees and grass

but this is a people paradise
where we are the creatures mostly
though thank God for dogs, cats, sparrows, and roaches.

This vertical place is no more an accident
than the Himalayas are.
The city needs all those tall buildings
to contain the tremendous energy here.
The landscape is in a state of balance.
We do God's will whether we know it or not:
Where I live the streets end in a river of sunlight.

Nowhere else in the country do people
show just what they feel—
we don't put on any act.
Look at the way New Yorkers
walk down the street. It says,
I don't care. What nerve,

to dare to live their dreams, or nightmares,
and no one bothers to look.

True, you have to be an expert to live here.
Part of the trick is not to go anywhere, lounge about,
go slowly in the midst of the rush for novelty.
Anyway, beside the eats the big event here
is the streets which are full of love —
we hug and kiss a lot. You can't say that
for anywhere else around. For some
it is the sex part they care about and get —
there's all the opportunity in the world if you want it.
For me it is different:
Out walking, my soul seeks its food.
It knows what it wants.
Instantly it recognizes its mate, our eyes meet,
and our beings exchange a vital energy,
the universe goes on Charge
and we pass by without holding.

Being Jewish

My mother's family was made up of loving women.
They were, on the whole, bearers,
though Esther, the rich sister, had only one,
she was the exception.

Sarah, the oldest, had five with her first husband,
(that was still in Poland),
was widowed and came here
where she married a man with four of his own,
and together they had another five,
all of whom she raised, feeding them in relays,
except little Tillie who sat in the kitchen
and ate with everyone, meaning all the time,
resulting in a fat figure
that made her despair of ever finding a husband,
but miraculously she did,
for God has decreed there is someone for everyone,
if you're desperate enough
and will take what you can get.

Aunt Rachel had twelve, raising them in a stable.
She was married to a junk dealer
who kept horses to haul the wagons.
He was famous for his stinginess
so they lived in a shack surrounded by bales of hay.
That was in America, in a slum called Bronzeville
that the black people have now inherited from the Jews,
God help them.
Then, as now, plenty of kids turned out bad,
going to work for that Jewish firm, Murder Incorporated,
or becoming junkies like one of my cousins did.

My mother only had six
but that's not counting... I'll say no more
than she was always pregnant,
with a fatalistic "What can you do?"
("Plenty," her friend Blanche replied—she was liberated.
"You don't have to breed like a rabbit.")
Like her mother who had a baby a year in Poland
until Grandpa left for America
giving her a rest.
There were women who kept bearing
even then, mysteriously, as from habit.

Women were always tired in those days and no wonder,
with the broken-down bodies they had
and their guts collapsed,
for with every child they got a dragging down.
My mother finally had hers
tied back up in the hospital and at the same time
they tied those over-fertile tubes
which freed her from "God's terrible curse on women."

And not just the bearing, but the work:
The pots couldn't be big enough for those hungry broods—
Sarah used hospital pots for hers.
And then the problem of filling the pots,
getting up at dawn to go to the fishing boats
for huge fish carcasses cheap,
buying bushels of half-spoiled vegetables for pennies,
begging the butcher for bones,
and then lugging it all home on their bad legs.
They didn't think of their looks for a minute,
and better they didn't, shapeless as that life made them.
(And yet they remained attractive to their men,
by the evidence of their repeated pregnancies.)

They just went around wrecks, always depressed,
unable to cope, or hiding in bed
while the children screamed.
"Escape, escape, there must be escape"
was my mother's theme song, until at last
her children escaped from her and her misery,
having wrecked her life, that endless sacrifice,
for what?

I see the proletarian women like them on the streets,
cows with udders to the waist
lugging black oilcloth shopping bags,
the mamales, the mamacitas, the mammies,
the breeders of the world with loving eyes.
They sit around the kitchen table with full hearts
telling each other their troubles—
never enough money, the beasts their men were to them,
the sorrow life was for a woman, a mother,
the children turning out no good—
and fed each other pieces of leftover meat from the ice box
to make up a little for life's pain
and sighing, drank tea
and ate good bread and butter.

Roaches

An old decrepit city like London
doesn't have any.
They ought to love it there
in those smelly, elegant buildings.
Surely I myself have smuggled some in in my luggage
but they obviously don't like the English—
for that alone I should love them.

They are among the brightest
and most attractive of small creatures
though you have to be prepared
for the look of horror
on the faces of out-of-town guests
when a large roach walks across the floor
as you are sipping drinks.
You reach out and swat,
and keeping the conversation going
pick up the corpse and drop it into an ashtray
feeling very New Yorky doing it.
After all, you've got to be tough to live here—
the visitor didn't make it.

Roaches also thrive on it here:
They set up lively communes
in open boxes of rice, spaghetti, and matzohs.
You come in to make coffee in the morning
and find a dead one floating in the kettle
and dots of roach shit on the dishes,
hinting at roachy revels the night before.

If you let them alone
they stop running at the sight of you

and whisker about
taking a certain interest in whatever you are doing,
and the little ones, expecting like all babies to be adored,
frolic innocently in the sink,
even in daytime when grownup roaches rest
after a night of swarming around the garbage bag.
The trouble with this approach is
they outbreed you and take over,
even moving sociably right into your bed.

Which brings up the question, Do they bite?
Some say yes, and if yes,
do they carry oriental diseases?
Even though you have tried to accept them
there comes a point when you find your eyes
studying labels of roach killers on supermarket shelves,
decide to try a minimal approach, buy one,
but when you attack with spray can aimed
they quickly learn to flee.
The fastest of course live to multiply
so they get cleverer all the time
with kamikaze leaping into space,
or zigzagging away,
race into far corners of the apartment
where they drop egg-sacks in their last throes
and start ineradicable new colonies.

When you light the oven
they come out and dance on the hot stove top
clinging with the tips of their toes,
surviving by quick footwork until you swat them.
Or if you spray it first
you have the smell of roaches roasting slowly.

And when you wash them down the drain
without their being certifiably dead
do they crawl up when the coast is clear?
Some even survive the deadliest poisons devised by man
and you have weird, white mutations running about.
Dying, they climb the walls, or up your legs, in agony,
making you feel like a dirty rat,
until they fall upside down with frail legs
waving in the air.

No more half-measures—
it's them or us you finally realize
and decide on nothing less than total fumigation:
The man comes while you are out
and you return to a silent apartment, blissfully roach-free.
You vacuum up the scattered bodies of the unlucky,
pushing down guilty feelings, lonely feelings,
and congratulate yourself.

                                               You booby,
they have only moved over to the neighbor's
and she too is forced to fumigate,
and just when you are on the princess phone crowing to your
        friends,
back they come, the whole tribe of them,
many gone now
due to their trivial life-span and chemical adversaries
but more numerous then ever with the new born
and all the relatives from next door and the neighborhood
        with them,
you standing there outraged, but secretly relieved
as they swarm into the kitchen from every crevice,
glad to be home, the eternal innocents,
greeting you joyfully.

Plant Poem

The shrimp plant on my desk had one long low branch
that moved mysteriously about,
turning to the sunlight outside
or, on dark days, toward the electric light inside.
You could actually see it travel with a kind of trembling.
Even when the sun was out
it might move across the table
and look right up at me where I sat.
It was like having a little friend, a pet.

I thought maybe the vibration of my typing
gave it the energy to do that.
Sometimes it moved and sometimes not,
it didn't always have the strength,
but the leaves could always swivel toward the light.
Finally it grew so long it got in my way
and in a merciless moment
I tied it upright to a stake.

I never again felt it looking at me.
I wonder if it was struggling to get free.

After the Moonwalk

When they landed on the moon
what we really wanted
was for strange creatures to seize them.

We wanted them to take off their helmets
and discover they could breathe,
that science was wrong
and there was air there.

We wanted people to be there,
tiny people who got that way
because they failed to develop usefully
and finally were banished
into a universe of rejected experiments.
And insects, perhaps the giant ancestors
of our own ants and bees.

When they took the first step on the moon
we wanted green insect men with mandibles and pincers
to rush out and right on television
drag them off to glass-enclosed cities,
or to underground factories and mines
where a humanoid race toils
that once ruled the moon
but invented nuclear weapons and destroyed it
and are now the slaves of giant ants who took over—
all this revealed before our eyes—
and an appeal for funds
to build a fleet of airships to attack the moon
and rescue our astronauts in captivity.

Instead what happened

was more like the way we once came to this continent
seeing nothing of value in the lives of the people here
and ruined them and their world,
like a renegade cell invading
(though surely the cancer cell obeys laws
that are still beyond our understanding).
What we left on the moon, the first gift of mankind,
was a pile of garbage.

If the moon was an egg
and the astronauts sperm-germs burrowing in
and if we chose them right for the task
(which I doubt, all white and macho as they were,
with those degenerate vibrations),
even so, it may be the beginning of a new world.

Our earth-probe succeeded
in breaking through the moon's defenses
destroying forever what it was,
but opening a path for settlers,
colonies of infection, the beginning of life

And if it isn't yet a living world in our sense
(though what in the universe is dead—it's all alive),
we have sent the germ cells of our biosystem
to start multiplying there.
Even now air seeds may be growing
an atmosphere like ours.

And when it is ready to be on its own
to search for its own orbit,
what great wrenching away is ahead
and dislocations of the stars,
tidal waves and firestorms on earth,

repeating the destruction of continents
when the moon was born like a baby from our oceans.

What was begun—and it began long ago,
the necessity for a moon—
must continue to the end,
with us sitting as long as we can,
glued to our TV sets,
watching it all.

A Visitation

The man fell out of the sky
crumpling among the dunes,
his legs and wings broken.

I saw him from the lighthouse window and ran out
calling Reina to come
and we brought him indoors
to the big room below.
He was surprisingly easy to carry.

Reina knew how to set broken legs
but how do you do wings?
Lying on his back as he was
they stuck out crookedly.
How do you lie down with wings on?
Wherever he came from
there must be special beds
or racks they hang over.

I started to call the doctor
but hung up, thinking
that this man with wings
could upset people a lot.

He stirred and mumbled blurry words.
Reina wiped off his face —
he was beautiful.
His eyes opened — they were blue.
He spoke, and we loved him.

What did he say?
Later on we talked about it a lot

but never agreed exactly
except that he called me brother
and Reina daughter
perhaps because between men
it is brotherhood that moves the heart
and for a man it is his daughter
who arouses his tenderness.

On awakening he had a kind of epileptic fit:
A vibration went through him
and his limbs healed instantly.
Maybe what we call epilepsy
is powers of the body
we don't know how to use.
He sat up, stretched his wings
that folded naturally behind him,
then leaned back against them.
Of course, that's the way you do it.

Our instinct had been right
not to tell anyone about him:
He thanked us for our kindness
and asked us not to give him away
for there would be no escaping the protective custody
earthmen would put him under.

He made a strange whistle,
a humming surrounded our lighthouse,
and we seemed to fall into trance.
I think a ship descended and there was activity.
Then we awoke, looking at each other with wonder.

The Drought

A strange wind came,
a dehydrating wind.
First they noticed a prickling on the face.
Then the plants wilted
and watering didn't help much—
the wind continued to blow
and dried everything up.
It was as though the air
lacking water
sucked all moisture into itself,
completed itself with water.
It was not just a desert wind,
it was a wind that devoured our substance,
for aren't we mostly liquid?

In no time the city was a dust bowl,
the survivors minimally there,
the few who could live like lizards,
the hardshelled ones preserving
a core of moisture in themselves,
a cactus race that grew spines
so that others like them
wouldn't devour them whole
for the sour fluid they contained.
That stinking fluid was life
and when two of them coupled
(one victoriously shooting his precious drops
into the insides of the other),
following this he died
having spent what he could—
one had to sacrifice himself
by yielding up his juice.

On those drops the other fattened,
a parasite in the belly.
But often small creatures would crawl in
and drink the fetus up
so that no child was born into the dust
but a monster grew
that gradually devoured the mother from within,
who thought it was a child
until she swelled from the gases and the rot
and burst like a dry puffball
in the arid air.

The wind blew that way for a time
and one day it changed back again.
Rain fell, things dampened and grew green.
Seeds burst their dry shells and flowered.
What seemed cactus turned feathery and creaturely.
Lizards turned inside out,
swelled with water and became cuddly.
As their scales fell off
turning from lizard to human,
as beaks turned to lips
people cried
remembering how hard it had been to survive
and how they had treated each other — ruthlessly.

But there were some
who had grown such a hard shell in the dry season,
their bones atrophied
and when the wind blew wetly again
could not give up their shells.
While others did soften, becoming plump and boneless,
desirable as sex objects
for the sadistic and egotistical Hard Shells.

Sometimes their brains would develop frighteningly,
the more helpless they were, the bigger the brain,
but their hardshell masters could kill them for sport, and did,
for Softies, as they were called, although rapable on whim,
were not considered quite human.

Did the Softies rebel? They did.
Not against the rape part, they liked that,
but against the sadism above and beyond sexual necessity,
and the senseless killing.
Yet who could win that long war
that tore apart the world for a generation?
When the drought was over we thought peace had come
        at last.
It brought a sudden increase in population
and then a slaughter.

The Softies had their brains
and the Hard Shells their hardness,
and the Others, well the others were glad
to see the freaks killing themselves off
and used each side as it proved expedient,
until the Softies and Hard Shells,
in cosmic paradox, joined forces
and attacked the Others,
not wiping them out of course
but leaving the odder members to survive and propagate.
Mankind does get odder and odder.

So the human race goes, in wet or dry.
Every disaster brings out new variations in us.

Burbank demonstrated the whole history of a plant
in its pod. He scattered the seeds

and grew all its generations in one season—
tough-skinned from drought, thorny from years of famine,
big from the easy time, small from cold.
Every period brought a change that was never forgotten,
memory in the seed.

If human history is a horror story,
it's all stored inside us, we're capable of it all.
Now who can predict what is coming, and what it will
        demand?
In the face of the future, prepared for any event
nature throws her million tricks—us.

Say the time comes when nothing we call good
could possibly survive—
to grow a skin of thorns to live,
is it worth it?

The Reservoir

The ancient reservoir,
an underground lake beneath the city,
has been closed to the public by the government
due to stringent budget cuts.

The news fills me with dismay.
It was the only thing I cared about
in that city of minarets, domes, and ruined palaces.
And to think I could have seen it
but passed it by, dismissing it
as a minor tourist attraction, not worth
spending fifteen minutes or fifty cents on.

I suppose there was nothing much to it:
You could go out on it in a boat,
though never all the way.
Imagine a city having a source of sweet water under it,
not needing aqueducts or to use the polluted river.

And maybe even it was a city underground,
now flooded, as the sewers of modern Jerusalem
once were Roman streets.

Too late I realize it was one of the important things.

It was closed for centuries
before being rediscovered and opened again.
And even if the population
never thought or even knew about it
still its presence must have affected them.
Like a desert is an energy accumulator,
a mountain a magnetic pole,

bodies of water give off an exciting influence.

Now it is shut again
and those carved pillars of limestone
that stretch away into the gloom
may collapse and the whole thing fill up with garbage,
become a sewer instead of a reservoir,
that underground lake, sacred to dervishes,
lost track of, and profaned.

And for how long, O my people,
I cry from the bottom of my wretched heart,
will it still be possible to reopen it, and explore?

To the Sikh Master, Kirpal Singh

Master, when I heard you speak
I couldn't understand,
it was all a mumble through your beard.
Is it if you are meant to be a disciple
you understand?

I could hardly see a gleam from your eyes,
they were in shadow.
Is it if you were meant to be my master
I would see loving eyes?

Master, when you looked at me
as you did for a second when leaving the room
it did not say, Come be my disciple,
but nothing special
like, Who are you? or What do you want?

I am no disciple, Master, I know.
Secretly, in my foolishness,
I want you to recognize me as your master,
I want you to look at me and proclaim,
Here is a higher being — and bow to me.

Someone must have a key to all my locked places,
those tight shoulders and sore calves,
my stuck breather, bad back, choking throat —
but if you do not
then I am still master of my closing up,
still seeking a master of opening up,
the master who will teach me how to let it all go
and help me face the terror of that release.
But seeing you, I couldn't believe

you were the one to do that for me.

I had a dream about you
in which you asked me for a light
but my match could barely light your cigarette:

Master, Master, I am ashamed
to come to you
with such a weak flame.

The Impossibility of Finding a Guru

I passed a wizard who made
goldfish displays in an aquarium store.
He was born in the month of En-li,
Hebrew for "There is none."

I knew he knew the secret of making
small levitating boxes you can ride in.
He said something about no freeze yet this winter.
This confused me,
was there a code in the small talk?

So I asked him his natal sign
to see if we were compatible.
En-li, he answered me in Hebrew, I have none.

Are you my guru, I wanted to ask
but without my asking he had answered me,
though I refused to accept it until I woke
and said to myself, En-li, there is none.

The Buddha, Radiant

for Dr. Park

When the healer put his hands on me
practicing an ancient art of pressure-therapy
it seemed that he transmitted a message
that I saw as the Buddha,

and understood that the Buddha was not a person really
but a shape of inner space
—a re-shaping of inner space—
that heals from within,

that the statue we know so well
is not a figure to worship, an idol,
but a meditation tool, a system of healing,

that that seated pose,
in its proportions, in its balance,
is a harmonizing image in the mind and body
to free us from tension
and bring us grace.

Encompassing the sexes,
it has something of a large child
—the human being at its softest and most divine—
and also of the mother,
that tranquil image of tenderness—
not at all like Christ twisted in agony.

With the doctor's hands magnetic on me
I understood that words were unnecessary
(and in any case he did not speak my language),
for it is a teaching image,

a demonstration of not holding on anywhere
allowing the energies to flow,

that releases the awkward self
from its lopsided cage
into a fullness in every part,
becoming all roundnesses, all smiles,
as if you felt the idea, *Thy will be done,*
in your whole body,
purring with it like a cat.

We could not speak to each other, the doctor and I,
but I received this teaching and blessing through his hands
when into my mind came the Buddha, radiant.

The Teaching

How can I sleep
when my car is racing down the hill
out of control?

The Master tells his students not to sleep,
that to awaken is the goal,
so why don't I remember that
and trust the dream which obviously says,
Do not sleep.

Remember your death, he says,
which means you only have this life
to do it in, to wake up in,
this time around anyway —
but I'm so tired and want to sleep,
then going to sleep
I remember my death and awaken.

Usually just thinking of morning's
struggle to get up
will put me soundly to sleep,
but after a long day's driving
I can't let go of the wheel
or the wheel can't let go of me
and the car takes off down the slope
and I wake with a jolt.

No nerve to let it fly
I lie there calming my fear
(self-calming, another sin according to the Master)
which should not be calmed
if we faced our true predicament:

And let the car fly off the cliff edge,
me with it, screaming,
and risk all
and see what will happen.

Dying

A palmist said I have another fifteen years
but lately my heart line
has been developing a break at the heart meridian
and I suspect it will be sooner.
I look healthy but only I know
the tensions that are tearing me apart.

Every author ought to choose
a young healthy literary executor
with a long life line.
Nevertheless I refuse to write my will.
My papers are such a mess
maybe I'll just destroy everything.
But why not leave behind a mess—
whatever is left is junk.

The big problem of dying is how to.
I know it will be very painful to let go,
if not terrifying,
and I'll need someone there to help me,
somebody I can trust—
though when I think how I'm holding now
and won't trust anyone
to help me let loose the bonds of fear
then how can I expect the right person
to come along at the last minute I have on earth?

The way I was raised to think about it
you just get put in the ground, become fertilizer.
That's no help for now,
me nearly fifty with the break in my heart line
and not having opened the gate to immortality
except once in my twenties, and then not understood.
I am truly faced with an impossible task

being in the condition I'm in.

It's not that I'm not ready—or is willing the word?
But in some sense I'm neither ready to live or die
or to accept the death in life
that would free me now
and let me face the body's death, whenever it comes,
as simply as a candle going out.

Chopped Meat

There is no longer a sun king
    on top of the Aztec pyramids
but if there were one I would sing,
    come eat my enchiladas.

*

TO STANLEY MOSS

If you insist on writing poems
    about my haystacks
you will force me
    to build them better.

*

When the newspapers went out on strike
    we could only hope
        that the magazines
            would quickly follow.

*

Whatever the gurus say
sex is still the most fun of anything.

*

MY ROLE IN LIFE

I'm like a doctor at a resort —
most people are there for a good time
but some have jobs and are useful.

*

Trotting is the one movement
all men do alike
and everyone does correctly.

*

It is a thousand times more important
to learn how not to hurt your loved ones
than to spend a lifetime
alleviating the sufferings of mankind.

*

THE MANGO TREE IN THE GARDEN

It is like owning a piece of jungle,
stripey things among the leaves,
the vegetable equivalent of a tiger.

*

He threw himself
into the meat grinder of life
and came out
                chopped meat.

*

Marguerite said to me:
"When my mother died
it was as if all my life the moon was in the sky
and suddenly—no more moon."

*

The Buddha says
you cannot die
holding on anywhere.

*

Gurdjieff whispered to me in the kitchen,
Be more awake.

*

Being all here
is like subjecting yourself
to an intense tickling
you can't stand.

*

Prayer is tuning in to the blessings.
They are always there
    ready to be turned on like a shower.
In fact, the shower is a blessing.
    Get in and turn it on.

*

I threw myself
into the meat grinder of your love
and came out
                chopped meat.

*

You talk about whores?
They are being paid for it.
You are giving it away.

*

You are the product
of a thousand lifetimes

and all you can accomplish in this one
is very little

but to do even that
you have to work as hard as you can.

*

The first requirement
   of a lover
      is that he want you.

*

I've got your number:
If you could be raped
over your protests
you would know
you were really desired.

*

Tonight I feel
what I can only call
stuck with myself.

*

ON POETRY

1.

A path where the least effort
is returned a thousandfold,

where my least effort
has been returned
a thousandfold.

2.

The great leap

over the gap
between thinking of an idea
and writing it down.

3.

Some things you make happen
and some things you let happen.

4.

Mannerisms
do not make it poetry

5.

If poetry is a refuge for snobs
any poet turning out human
is in the nature of a miracle.

*

AFTER MASTURBATION

That wave of pleasure —
no further justification
is necessary for it.

*

Hello, Snow

*

SANCHO

Leaping up to lick your face
he waved his golden tail.

He would never disappoint you
by not being happy in your presence.

*

As the smile is to the face
the hard-on is to the body.

*

CAB RIDE

How I agonize,
watching the meter rise.

*

NOON

The tree
is in the center
of its shadow.

*

Waves of my love
go out to him.
Surely he feels it!

*

Holding the hands together
palm to palm in front of you —
self-recognition of your whole being.

*

AT THE WESTERN WALL

O Lord, thank you
for bringing me back
to Israel once more.

*

HOW TO COPE: *The Echo Principle*

How do you do it?
                    ...you do it.
How do you go on?
                    ...you go on.

*

DECREE: *From a Plane above the Clouds*

With the authority invested in me
by the people of the United States of America
and the Congress thereof,

I hereby declare this
CLOUDS NATIONAL PARK.

Unwanted: A Villanelle

In spite of all the attention I get
I'm sure that nobody wants me:
You are what you are and I am unwanted.

You wake up in the morning and go about your day
not even dreaming or caring that I exist—
in spite of all the attention I get.

You are involved in the latest fashions
in literature or love, and why not?
You are what *you* are, and I am unwanted.

I want everyone to talk about me all the time,
even more than they do, and no one to mind,
in spite of all the attention I get.

I don't want to work for it, strive for it, sing for it.
If God meant me to have it, it would all come to me:
You are what you are and I am unwanted.

Give me pills, a fistful of daggers, the pipe from the gas jet—
I just don't want to go on living any more
in spite of all the attention I get.

Somehow what you are is obvious from the start: Everyone
        knows.
The soul has its rating, and mine's zero.
In spite of all the attention I get,
you are what you are and I am unwanted.

Diary: October 11, 1972

On some days everything goes bad:
The car doesn't pass inspection, no mail comes,
it seems nobody loves me—anyway
everybody passes by without saying,
Stay with me forever,

but instead they go on down the street
to their own lives
and I stand there wishing a truck would stop
and the man would lean over and say, Hi, hop in.

Yes, and my lumbago hurts, reminding me
that my pains are my own responsibility—
nobody else is doing that to me—
and not the fault of the car inspector
or the indifferent truckdriver.

Look, what's so terrible about your life
that you should do this to yourself?
I hate it, that's what.
Who has the strength for the day-to-day of it?
Take care of somebody else, yes,
but to have to pay attention to yourself? Ugh.

That's why I need somebody on such a day
and nobody comes, nobody is simply there.
Where are you, difficult darling?
Maybe it has to be someone of a special type
that is very rare, and maybe
there is only one of them in the whole world
besides me, and the chances of meeting him
are infinitesimal,

somebody as hard to find as a guru
you have to walk around the Himalayas looking for.
Though as a holy man once said,
it is not enough for you to love God,
God must love you too.
The seeker must be sought.

I know what the I Ching would say to all this,
Get back in tune with the universal order of things,
stop fighting whatever is happening,
even this downward negative spiral.
And if you can't smile, then sigh,
one of those deep Jewish sighs that say,
This is how things are going in the universe today, rotten,
and all is as it should be.

The Gods Desert Antony

after Cavafy

I stand by my window looking over this valley.
　There is a sad music in the air
for when the gods desert you
　they play a music that we feel as grief.
Antony heard it too one night in Alexandria
　when he was king, and for queen
　he had Cleopatra, that delicious woman,
　as I had you, dear one.
What a city that was to be king of.
Then he heard the music of those rascally gods
　masquerading as a band of minstrels
　as those wise ones, those friends, foretold.
And at that moment, did he weep?
　Did he rage at the gods
　for depriving him of such a paradise?
Yes, he wept, he raged,
for you do not give up such a life
　without tears and cursing.
You do not act noble, standing on the hill
　outside the city
　and wave goodbye to the Alexandria you are losing.
No, you tear your clothes in mourning
　and go wailing through the world, alone,
alone forever perhaps, forever probably,
　and never forgive, certainly never forget,
for the kingdom had become your soul
　and without it now you are nothing.

Kabul, 1971

The Lost, Dancing

after Cavafy

When the drums come to your door
do not try to shut them out,
do not turn away and resist them,
for they have come to tell you what you need to hear,
they are your fate.
When Antony heard them
he knew then that he had lost Egypt forever.
He did not shriek or tear his clothes
for he always knew they would come someday.
What the drums speak to you
is so inevitable you have to agree with them—
nothing else could be right.
So when the drummers and dancers come to your door
your life changes,
and with no bitterness
but with a sad smile
—after all what you had you had,
you loved the way few men love—
and as someone who was worthy of such a kingdom,
join the army of the lost, dancing,
follow the drums
and turn and wave goodbye
to the Alexandria you are losing.

*Rio de Janeiro
Carnival, 1974*

42

The Book of Sorrow

This notebook, empty.
What shall be written in it?
It is waiting for the words of pain,
the life to come without my dear one.
The record of a wanderer without a home.
So many pages and each
a day of loneliness.
How long can this go on?
After this book is filled
there will be another, and another,
and another....
The story of my life.

Open Sesame

The door in the rock closed
just as he was about to enter.
His fingers even left imprints in the stone
where he gripped the panels,
straining against them
as they slid together.

A minute more
and he would have gotten in.
Now he is almost embedded in the rock,
arms outstretched
across the seamless face of it.

Ant

An ant walks on the window screen
looking for a hole big enough to get through.

He walks for what must seem miles
looking at the endless holes. He goes back and forth

convinced that one of the holes
must be bigger than the others

but the screen is new
and all the holes are the same size.

The Farewell

They say the ice will hold
so there I go,
forced to believe them by my act of trusting people,
stepping out on it,

and naturally it gaps open
and I, forced to carry on coolly
by my act of being imperturbable,
slide erectly into the water wearing my captain's helmet,
waving to the shore with a sad smile,
"Goodbye my darlings, goodbye dear one,"
as the ice meets again over my head with a click.

The Ghetto

for Arthur Gregor

A child devoted to sacred study, pale,
his whole life this, and prayer, and ritual,
looked up one day and saw a dragonfly,
went out and followed it, not knowing why,
through the ghetto shrouded in mystery and awe.

He climbed the walls surrounding it and saw
the world outside, and jumped without a thought
for those he left behind and what they taught:
that the life of play and foolish laughter is,
for all of that, no happier than his.

Without a choosing to or not to, he was out
and saw the hills, smelled hay, heard children shout,
and ran, his head uncovered, through fields of flowers
and fell in the grass and lay there overpowered.

Passover Meditation

1.

The world needs a certain amount of suffering to survive
and somebody's got to do it.
So if the Jews are spared another holocaust
other people will have to make up for it—
that seems to be the Law.

No one will voluntarily be mankind's scapegoat—
who accepts tragedy willingly?
They'll blame the Jews for displacing it from themselves
and make us pay.

Before it was the Germans, now it is the Arabs.
Jews are no different from anyone else,
we want to escape our destiny of suffering
but the world will never let us, for long.
They know whose role that is.

And we know it too, and that knowledge
leaves us with a feeling of worthlessness
as well as the feeling that we're special.

From the beginning Jews refused
to bow to cosmic purpose
which mostly meant accepting our load of misery,
so our history was shaped
by protests against fate
and being difficult about it.
Who could blame us for that?

We don't accept, though Buddhists counsel this.
Thy will be done is for Christians and Moslems,
who seem to have their own idea
of what God's will is for us,

so we take it right in the *kishkas* again and again
and go down complaining.

2.

When the climate changed in our land
and rain did not fall and there was famine,
we went to Egypt
where they knew how to farm without rain.

The Pharoah welcomed us as a holy people
and even married one of our women, a prophetess,
and when in time their children married each other, as was
        the custom,
and ruled the land
they installed a new religion of one God
with our people as teachers,
deposing the ancient priesthood.

Of course the priests got back in power eventually
and the Jews had to pay:
We were accused of taking over the government
and for centuries considered as subversives,
suffered under the lash as slaves.

3.

The years of our captivity
    were Egypt's most brilliant.
When we left, its decline began.

For though we had labor forced on us,
  like building those damn pyramids,
the upper classes were exempt
  and brought Egypt
the sophistication only Jews had then:

the freedom for women unheard of in that world
  and respect for the arts,
not to mention an idea
  that would rescue mankind again and again:
that God is One.

And when we saw our way clear to escape,
  a man of vision appeared
who led us away from that nightmare world
  of a great culture gone mad.
And on leaving, our people
  under a brilliant leadership
destroyed the Egyptian army

and that, plus the departure
  of the best Jewish/Egyptian intellectuals,
wrecked Egypt in its soul
  ending the Golden Age—
for genius follows
  where holy energy is.

A nation left Egypt
  took back our ancient land
and with the secrets of agricultural science
  learned in Egypt
made it the richest land in the world.

4.

There is no hint of any of this in Egyptian history.
It is nearly all of our history.

They wiped it out of their memory forever.
We remember it forever.

Our people didn't set out to destroy Egypt
but having done so, it couldn't be forgiven

and even centuries of slavery there
wasn't enough justification.

You do what you must, rejoice when it succeeds,
and pay the price forever.

Then, having reached a certain stage of being,
they received the teaching, the ten sacred rules,

and a holy city that was such a treasure
peace would never come to them

for everyone would always want it for their own
and indeed that's what happened

and we were scattered across the earth
especially among the cruelest peoples of mankind

the white Christians of Europe
who finally horrified even themselves with their evil

—all the universe was horrified—
so that our country was returned to us

along with that city like a treasure, though a curse,
that will never allow us to be at peace

though peace is there
in the eye of the hurricane.

5.

The world is beginning to understand
how much we love our land.
The Arabs still do not understand this
or refuse to.
They say we are not of that land
but our memories are longer than theirs:
Though we seem modern
and love the modern
we are more traditional even than Moslems
who have exalted tradition.

It does not matter where we are born
we do not forget our land.
What is a few thousand years away?
We have lost it before, many times,
driven into slavery, exile,
from before history.

Kick us out
and we find our way back:
It is the meaning of our lives to do so.

Without Israel
our lives have no meaning.

And if there is no Israel
our lives won't mean anything.

Addressed to Angels, Not Humans

Praise the name of Hitler and rejoice
for it was by his hand
that brought such a misfortune to the People
that the Lord felt compassion for them again at last,
after so many centuries of sorrow, of wandering,
and let them return, the remnant,
to their home in Israel once more.

Both My Grandmothers

Both my grandmas came from far away
on the difficult journey alone with their children.
They had the courage to do that
but only enough strength
to get here, raise their kids, and die.
I myself have stood on the shore of the Caspian Sea
crying my eyes out
and know how far away far can be
and how far this America — strange and difficult even
        for me —
was from their homes,
from the life they yearned back to.
But they lived here uprooted the rest of their lives.

You died, dear ones, not knowing
that your grandson loved you
and would remember you one day when he was fifty
and need you, and wish, my angels, you were there.
Eat, eat, *tottele,* you would say
if you saw me crying now.
For you were so humble
you could not believe you had anything else to offer.
And maybe eating is life's one reliable consolation
after all the disappointments
and the anguish of your children's lives.

You are long gone, my grandmas, darlings.
People are so fragile
and it is impossible to protect our dear ones
from the terrible things that happen to them,
that we do to them.
Our fate seems always to lose

our homes, our loved ones, forever.
But, my little mothers, I must tell you
that this year I went to Jerusalem, our golden city.
How you would have loved it there
in our homeland, where the heart is full.
Even if it was denied you in your lifetimes
I know that's where your spirits went when you died.
For surely that is what called me there,
not you alone, but all our ancestors are there—
they have returned to The Land, our land.

Help me, courageous ones, help me
stand up for my people, for Israel, for myself,
although frankly I feel a man is not worth anything.
Only as a Jew perhaps am I worth anything.

I know when I think of you, my grandmas,
that you are the connection with my ancestors
whom I have somehow lost.
How did the energy line get broken?
When you crossed the sea?
When I grew up an American, different from my father
but as he wanted me to be,
not speaking his heart's language or knowing the
        synagogue?
So I go on crying all my life,
for you, for me, for my ma,
still afraid of the dark, afraid of the man who will come
        get me,
and most of all afraid of the power in me
that life has not used.

I won't ever forget you again.

Both of you are with me now, and through you, my people.
I have the strength of all of you,
even in sorrow, and defeat.

Thanks to you, I know who I am.

Nostalgie du Pays

Is there a spring in a quiet valley somewhere,
perhaps a farm that has been deserted
where the trees have not quite retaken the fields
but the overgrown pasture now has bramble patches in it
and hills rise around with their ragged third-growth forest?

And in that valley is there a spring
bubbling up out of the grasses
and a thin stream flowing away from it?

And ruins of the farmhouse somewhere near
with broken pottery and jars in the collapsed cellar?
Everywhere the noise of insects and birds,
little animals lurking around the remains
of lilac bushes, outhouse, and rhubarb patch?
And tart, wormy fruit dropping in the neglected orchard?

People once came and cut down the forest,
made a farm in the wilderness
and lived here for a while,
then left mysteriously for other lives.
Now what remains
the vegetable kingdom is taking back again,
dimmer and dimmer the echoes of the human interval.
But before it all disappears forever under dark trees
I want to say, I was there in late autumn,
I was there.

In Memoriam

for Jean Garrigue

The wind that blew by me
will be different forever

Here where I drift in a boat on the lake
it rose
moved my boat a little
and all was still again

It went on
reshaped by my shape
and blew the leaves of the woods
differently after me

Had it not been for me being here
the wind would not have stirred dead leaves
felled twigs
in exactly that way
shifted bugs
to new environments
or changed the path of birds

In fact the universe
will never be the same again
and the course of my life too
has been utterly changed by that breeze

Beside A Pool

In the pool
there are polliwogs
so there must be something else here,
something that eats the polliwogs,
or maybe nothing bothers to eat polliwogs.
Come on, you know something is eating those polliwogs.
Nothing's too insignificant to be eaten,
like who'd think anyone would bother
to eat sunflower seeds — you crack
and there's hardly anything there
but a mouthful of shells.   .
Still, half the world is seed-eaters
and the other half lives off the seed-eaters,
those innocents. Really,
you have to be half-innocent at least
to eat seeds by the hour.
I sit here by the pool where the polliwogs wiggle
and tiny ants are eating me
not to speak of landlord, government, gnats, and devils:
Nobody's too insignificant to be eaten.

The Sand Map

I am looking for the places
    that were there before the sand.

What is strange about this country,
    sphinxes and pyramids on a duny plain,
        is what emerges from the hidden.

Once they looked ordinary in their real setting,
    not desert, but a green,
        a populated world,

and now covered by sand
    its peaks are hints
        we try to make sense of,
            imagining we long for it.

We long for something all right
    and dream of finding a sand map to lead us there
        hoping that under the desert is where it is.

If not that, what are we longing for?
    What lost world? But what if
        it is for something new, not old,
            the not-yet-born?

And even with a sand map, an accurate one,
    say you follow it, trustingly,
        and discover that buried world
            with its glories, and horrors,

then what do you have?
    Even knowing what was there,

following a program of limited excavation
   won't bring it back,

won't make sands that cover it blow away,
   make those figures on friezes come to life,
   and the cataclysmic scenes replay.

For after you have found it,
   after all that searching and working,
     you'll have to look at your life and see
      that nothing has changed—

so, having dealt with the past as best you could
   you might declare it is better
     to know than not to know,

but having used up the best of your strength,
   weary now, you must live with what you are,
     and even if it is desert, where you are,
      making the best of it.

The Celebrity

You thought the sad and lonely little boy
would go away if you ignored him

but it doesn't matter how old you get
or how famous or skilled in your art
he'll be there waiting.

Now that you've done in life
what has made you successful and adored
you find that none of it matters
and a terrible misery possesses you.
For what you were doing
was creating a false person,
that grown-up professional you are not at home in.

But the little boy doesn't want any of that.
Ask him what it is he wants.
It will not be easy to let him speak, or to listen—
he's no intellectual.
Nor will he be talked out of his feelings.

If you still have hope
that you might be rescued from this anguish you feel,
that somehow you could avoid it
by filling up your days, finding love,
it's too late for that.
Unless you deal with him at last
your life won't work.

You have to get to know him again
and take care of him,
that little boy who needs there to be a God

and who loves Lana Turner movies,
and above all, in spite of being worthless,
has a right to be loved.

All the years are falling away
with the illusion of youth that believes
we can become what we want.
Your misery is no mystery:
It's his old misery that you stifled.
You're still that little boy.

Football With the Sound Turned Off

As basketball players love leaping
and the sound of the ball swishing through the net,
football players love the ground,
crashing against each other and falling
into body piles.

On an immense field, watched by millions,
the tackle reaches out for the runner,
pulling him down.
Then, camera up close, the whole team
falls on top, lying there body on body
until at a signal
they untangle in slow motion.

The ball they use can only be caught
by hands magnetized to the odd roundness of it,
a perfect fit, just as they cannot resist
patting each others'
smoothly uniformed behinds.

With their bodies they batter their way
through a field of obstacles,
flesh bruising flesh, colliding
with electric shocks of feeling
that they must fling aside
to strive for the victory of a lonely touchdown.

Playing by rules, with referee on field
and coaches, managers, and owners
sitting on guard on the sidelines,
they still snatch moments of the forbidden
when after a score the camera eye slides away

from the players hugging and the slapping of asses
to the bleachers with their milling fans.

Watching this body ballet with the sound off,
long shots giving in to close-up views,
the shocks pulse through me
as bodies meet in violent contact,
my appetite judging my life and world,
deprived of the real and necessary
touching each other that we hunger for.

The Two Orders of Love

We have every right to hate them, he said,
looking at the girl nestling against the handsome head
of the blond giant in the row in front
of us sitting in our separate seats.
And sometimes it does seem
they have all the breaks.

In most places, outside the big cities,
even our men feel compelled to go with them—
you feel so out of it otherwise—
and except for a handful of rebellious young,
we shrink from contact with each other in public
as though by some repellent chemistry.

It is only fear.
If our longing could be expressed
we too would be hanging on each other's shoulders,
our lovers too would be profiled in doorways
and starred on the public grass of parks.

But for us it is forbidden,
not so much by law
as by a system of intimidation
not only of our actions but worse, of our feelings,
so that what we deny ourselves we persecute in others.

And they, our sisters, have the right
and are encouraged to enjoy
those empires of careless pleasure
we can only dream of, and pillage in haste, in secret,
or if we walk hand in hand, there is no ease in it.

We have every right to hate them and yet do not
because it is in its essence
a different thing we want, though it looks the same.
Nature needs both to do its work
and humankind, confusing two separate orders of love
makes rules allowing only one kind
and defies the universe.

David's Dream

*"You're not ready for
the convent yet."*—D.D.T.

He said that he dreamed
that everyone was meeting at the baths tonight
except me.
I'll be teaching there in the morning
so I couldn't go.

Well, he's got my number all right, I'm no fun.
I talk liberation
but my actions show otherwise,
and he dreams me as I really am,
a ruler-snapping nun
keeping the class in line.

My image is definitely bad.

I only show up at the baths
when morning guilt lights up the shabby linoleum
and the employees are scrubbing the love juice
off the walls and ceilings of the orgy room,
and the customers are putting on their jeans
anxious to go home.

That's when I arrive with my attendance book
and a sad sack stuffed with experience,
teaching what I don't believe in
and nobody wants to hear.

THE LESSON: If all you can do is teach
              don't do it at the baths.
        If you go to the baths
              don't go in the morning.

And if you go into the steam room
  take off your habit, baby,
  and leave your ruler home.

Street Instructions: At the Crotch

*"It is not against the law
to grope yourself."*—D.D.T.

"Remember yourself."—Gurdjieff

While walking toward housewife wheeling baby
reach down and squeeze your cock,
looking at her casually.

Adjust cock from left side to right
causing half hard-on
then shift it back.

Wear balls on one side, cock on other.

Tug at crotch of pants as if to free genitals
tangled in underwear.
Give it a good tugging.
Go out without underwear.

Make small tear in bulge of basket,
exposing skin.
Sew patch on crudely.

Wear pants of some material
flimsy as the law allows.

Go out with fly unzippered.
Go out with fly unbuttoned.
Break zipper and fasten with safety pin.
Rip crotch and sew with large jagged stitches.

While talking with friends
unzip fly, lower pants, and arrange shirttails.

Ask policeman for directions
and while he's telling you
give yourself a feel.

Walk loosely
to give yourself as much genital stimulation as you can.
Let it all move.
Be there.

Wearing My Nose

It takes a lot of nerve
to stick so far out in front
of your face.

It feels big
and hooked.
I wish my cock felt as big.

It is surely discussed behind my back.
I peek through one eye at the downward curve.
I study the hump.
I will it to be straight,
uptilted. Push it up with a finger—
It's hopeless.

Is it mostly to smell with?
Or to take the temperature of the space before you?
Or to poke inquisitively
into crevices and holes?

It provides passage to air in and drool out.
Rummaging inside
can reward with enchanting nuggets,
often with a comet trail of slime.

Wearing my nose while driving
I feel pug-nacious.

And the indignity of a fly landing on it.

Or a pimple emerging on it hotly.

There is sadness there
(it is odious), left over
from a childhood punch in the nose.
It is an accumulation, a whole history
of pain.
It is where I feel most humiliated,
like a shameful bundle I'm forced to carry around.

I prefer to imagine it is not there.
I will it not to be there.

But it shows.
And everyone knows.

In England

I can be quite happy here
though I never forget that I am in the land of the enemy.
The people have a deep antagonism toward me
whether they take me for a Jew or not.
They know Jew is not just a label.
Their fantasy that we control all the wealth
grows from a difference that is real.

When I look at one of them
he shrinks from my eyes, blinking hard,
or sometimes giving an involuntary jerk of the head.
He feels, why should he be subjected in his own country
to these foreigners who get too close,
who dare to look.

The English are not so rude as to look in your eyes
so they are easy to lie to
for they accept face value and do not read the heart,
just the manner and dress, the swagger or cringe.
Their ideal—the perfect lady or gentleman—
is civilized, calm, and coolly wise,
a presence to make everyone else unhappy
with his undignified farting humanity.

Their tight mouths and that pursy way of talking
are formed from a life of self-control:
For example, they are toilet trained
from as early as three days old.
So it should be no surprise to learn
that the noise most offensive to their ears
is the sound of children.

They torment their dogs
forcing them to conform to human standards of behavior
that are cruel even to humans.
And like all the rest of us
the dogs want to please and feel guilty when scolded
though they can't resist giving into pleasure
and can't remember at the moment of wanting
what is or isn't forbidden.
Running into flowerbeds is forbidden,
and shitting, and eating shit,
and worse, to grow excited is most forbidden
and leap and be loud.

They have contempt for the immigrant
Pakis, Wogs, and Blacks,
not to speak of the vassal Irish, Scots, and Welsh.
For Jews it is more like hatred.
The newspapers are full of sympathy
for Palestinian guerrillas
whereas they are indignant at their own
Irish independence fighters.

But they have taught me something important:
They reawaken in me the knowledge
that I am more oriental than western.
They are the epitome of the westerner.
They have a quality of bringing out in everyone
his racial identity
for their contempt is like a developing solution
to everything they despise:
Their presence defines the exact level
of your inferiority according to race.

It was not just the Empire
and being boss to half the world
that made them that way.
When the Jews were banished from England
some became Christians on the surface
and went on with their lives,
Jews being the world's great adapters.
But this didn't satisfy the church
and to escape the penalties, the hidden Jews
developed a style more English than the English.
It came out like snobbery
but was really terror—not to be found out—
and hatred—someone else's Jewishness
could expose your own,
resulting in the English upper classes of today
with their incredible sensitivity to all things Jewish.

Now centuries later, all that is resolved
into Fear of the Different
and Hatred of the Oriental.
So when I go there I don't expect them to love me.
I wear a falsely pleasant expression
which is all they demand—they don't want the real me—
and I look at them talking at each others' faces,
mutually secure that they will not be seen into.

If the dogs didn't want so much to be people
they would probably go crazy.

In the Can

We sit on a seat with a hole in it.
Below, the waters receive our shit.

Shit means to sit
and let it happen.
If you don't shit well
sit better and shit better.

Visiting a friend in the country
I saw a strange armchair in her living room
with a flap in the seat.
Curious, I raised the flap
and there was a tin box full of shit, piss, and tampax.

When you look at a Moslem or a Hindu
you know he has a clean ass:
Christians and Jews are dirty.

In our part of the world you sit,
in the East you squat.
Here you wipe with paper,
a brown smear.
There you wash your asshole
with your fingers.
There is often a water tap
or you bring in a pitcher of water,
the problem being to keep your clothes out of the way,
especially if you are wearing
the flowing clothes of those lands:
With one hand you hold your clothes in a bunch,
with one hand you pour the water,
and with another hand you wash your ass:

It's hard to do.

We are ashamed of our assholes,
a dark and dirty secret.
When I had piles
they got better when I talked about them:
The ass doesn't like to be ignored.

It is good to touch it.
It keeps you in touch with reality.
Feel the wrinkles, feel the hairs around,
feel the smooth lips,
slip in smoothly, feel the muscle of it.

This morning I shit
one of the great turds of all time.
It lay there, filling the bowl,
a perfect circle:

It was as if I had made a prayer.

Morning Song

Let a composer write a symphony
to the movements of his bowels.

I, huddled on my toilet seat,
have only this song to sing

on these mornings
when I cannot stop my shitting:

starting with the first foot-long
well-formed golden turd
circling the bowl

to the last dwindlings like string
tangled on the bottom

or sometimes a mushy pile
on the porcelain slope at the water's edge,

until there is nothing left to sing,
the bass notes end—
and the high ringing tones of hunger
with its own music comes.

Sonja Henie Sonnet

In high school we danced the lindy white-style
like Sonja Henie on her skates
curvetting her way around the rinky-dink
back-first, front-first, leaving a trail of scars.

Splitting in air or dissolving in a spin
she came out holding her muff to cheeks
dimpled and rosy under Bo-Peep bonnet
as snowflakes starred her blond and marcelled head,

and curtsying, her little behind
peek-a-booed under fluffy skirt
when she braked to a stop before the cameras
in a cloud of powdery ice.

Below, blunt feet in leather with blades of steel
dug in their points and held.

Pasternak: In Memoriam

Pasternak, I understand you now:
You were much too wise finally
to let politics interfere with your life.
You appreciated what a miracle it was
to be able to go on living at home in a world like ours
where everything threatens daily life —
invasions, wars, political purges.
You knew that the most important thing
is to stay real, at home, undisturbed,
to live quietly in comfort with a loved one,
daily routine, boring perhaps
but how deliciously, luxuriously boring —
that is all one dreams of
in the melodramatic times of revolution and war.
To lead such a life and then
to put it into jeopardy for principle?
You would have to be mad.
When the world takes it from you
is time enough to start acting symbolically.

Everyone wanted to use you,
even your friends, and they couldn't understand
your not standing up for your books
(that in any case were written and would live).
But when they threatened your daily life, those friends,
the life of the poet,
then they were your enemies, those stupid idealists.
Heroes are fools and there is time to be a hero perhaps.
Heroes have nothing to lose,
they have not learned to make a life in the world.
Survive, survive, the poet says.
What it comes down to is that in a world like this,

and after the horrors you lived through,
when you have found a corner to live peacefully in at last
you would be out of your mind
to risk it to change the world somehow, anyhow.

Let the people whose lives are insupportable
rise against their masters,
throw themselves on the barricades,
be their own heroes,
not ask you to be their hero.
They will have their Great Loves in those times,
loves they hardly make love with
and rarely if ever live with,
loves that are like life's promises
never to be fulfilled
but linger as heart-filling dreams
making the rest of your life drab forever—
who needs it?

You were right:
This real person in my arms
is who I want
not the moment of passion on the barricades
not the dream of the ideal
love in a perfect world.

Survive in this world
love as you can
and go on with your work.

Living With an Aries

They want to run away constantly—
this you must discourage,
but luckily they are easily discouraged by delay
for their nature is to act instantly
or their energies die.

They love little harmless lies invented on the instant
though the truth would do as well.
Indulge them in this. Resist correcting
the exaggerated versions of stories they tell,
or saying "we" which wrecks
the free-wheeling image they like to project.

They are ready for a love affair
every two weeks.
Pity their discarded lovers
and be glad you are just in the friend category:
You will last.
You can discourage them in their romantic fallacies
by criticism or better, ridicule.

The trouble is they live or they die
and there is no in-between.
Their ambitious plans can succeed amazingly
if they act at once, on the instant of conception,
or fail, but the important thing is
they live by action.

Nothing, nothing is more pitiful
than a crushed Aries, or a caged one.
Possess one to your peril, and theirs.
Don't be fooled by placidity:

Underneath is a volcano, ready to blow its stack.
If it doesn't, they develop alarming diseases
that only the movies could invent,
but on the brink of death
will recover miraculously —
teaching their would-be keepers
to let go, be content to look on
their mad head-on scramble for doing,
for a kind of life
anyone else would consider hell on earth
but which suits their natures.

How often can you batter a wall with your head
and live? You reason with them.
No use, they will continue
until one or the other gives.

So if you love, stand back and let them.
Your only consolation is this:
They will come to you for comfort sometimes.

Writing for Money

My friend and I have decided to write for money,
he stories, I poems.

We are going to sell them to magazines
and when the cash rolls in
he will choose clothes for me that make me stylish
and buy himself a tooth where one fell out.

Perhaps we will travel, to Tahiti maybe.
Anyway we'll get an apartment with an inside toilet
and give up our typing jobs.

That's why I'm writing this poem,
to sell for money.

Longing for Lee Poe

in homage to Tu Fu

Separated as we are by half a continent
    —but only a few hours by jet—
still my commitments prevent me
    from flying straight to you, dear friend.
How I long for you
    surrounded as I am by people
    who do not satisfy my soul.
The trouble with it here
    in the middle of the country where I am
is that it is all America
    in every direction for a thousand miles—

but it's not my America: You are that.
    You are also my China.
I long for the time I get home next week
    and I can cook you one of your favorite dishes:
    Noodles? Mashed potatoes? Shrimp Cantonese?
And I'll look into your dear eyes
    that know suffering now
    (how young they were when we first met)
    but also appreciate laughter as I do.
That's my happiness,

                    to be with you,
whatever insanity the world is into.

But for now I've got to suffer the Midwest plains,
    earning a living.

How I hate having to work for money.
   It should just be given for doing nothing,
   otherwise it can never be used properly,
for real pleasure. It is tainted by work.
And how I long for you, long to hold you,
   to look at your face.
I dream of our meeting again above all things, dear one.
   Wait, wait for me....

                    there you go,
disappearing into the past,
   half a continent turning into half a millennium
as you fade into history, a victim
   of the incredible time-machine we live in.
And I face how alone I am, another victim,
   far from home
and unable to summon you up in spirit or flesh.

To get to sleep I light my kif pipe
   and inhale deeply twice.

Gone Blind

He's a shrine, my blind friend at home.
Wherever I go, and I go far,
I remember him, and my heart is full.

Always he fills me with feeling
like someone far from home
who longs for his mother.

In his blindness I am at home
for I find in it my fullness.
In his helplessness—
and he is not practically helpless
but helpless as we all are,
to help ourselves—
my life becomes a frailty.

O to be there,
to put my arms around his sightlessness—
He has become so gentle now,
all arrogance gone
of one who makes demands on life.
In his gratitude for love
he shines with love.
In his victimhood he shines
like babies shine,
like women shine from their pain,
like saints and animals shine.

That he is not here with me is unthinkable.
Where have I lost him? Why is he not here?
O he is, here, in my heart.
He is my sacred figure, a shrine.

Gone blind
he has brought me light.

Visiting Home

It is an exercise in independence
not being like them.

Seeing that our bodies
are of the same nature
I religiously do my yoga
and stay open to other possibilities.

I remind myself I am allowed to shit.
So far I've been able to
though this morning I doubted.

Genital feelings nevertheless
are a long ways off.
They still have me by the balls.

My father and I suffer the same ailments:
electric leg in the night, back trouble
prima donna stomach,
a ringing in the left ear.

My mother declares her goal
is not to have to do anything
(that's me too)
and she refuses to make any effort
even to save her life.

We suggest activities
but all she wants is to go away on a greyhound bus,
live in hotels
and hang out in the lobby and cocktail lounge
talking to people.

Old ladies ought to be allowed.

I too am a roamer,
a talker with strangers,
but I have stars for travel
and she's stuck at home.

The trouble is she's one of the poor.
My father holds the purse strings
and it's as if he were still doling out to her
the daily allowance of five dollars
to feed the family on.
She will always believe in revolution
and be a feminist through and through.

By studying them
can I really know anything about myself?
But I can't stop.
Oh, all this concentrating for years
on what happened in childhood
to make me a mess,
all the analysis of transferences and dreams
to see how I repeat the defeat....
All that rebellion against being like them.

II

At lunch my father sits
hunched over his food
like some incredibly primitive
prehistoric man.

His face I feel as an unused
structure within my own. It is made
for glaring, raging, judging, criticizing.
I wish I could melt it down softer.

Under my mild looks
I have his skull, his features,
even his expression,
afraid of life, afraid of the flow.

We share an essential joylessness.
As I get older, that is starting to show
and it is a measure of our difficulties
that I will hate looking like him.

At the table he will hardly meet my eyes.
His slide away, masking a confusion of feelings.
Yet when I say I am going to leave
he gets a stricken look on his face.

My mother shyly kisses me
half on the lips. It is sweet.
I think of my grandmother's huge soft wet kisses,
messages from another world of feeling
where nothing is held back.

My mother's eyes are wide open.
We gaze at each other and love flows.
My father and I can't seem to find a way
to let that happen.

What if I said to him, Daddy—
though it would be better in Yiddish,
the language he can express himself in—

Daddy, I don't want to go on for the rest of my life
with this barrier between us.

I don't blame you for the past,
my hellish childhood, and the years after,
that nightmare, when I didn't know how to live my life.
Let's try to be straight with each other,
though there is no ignoring the wreckage between us.

But it is as if I were waiting for him to start,
as though he alone had the key to that door
to what feels like the possibility of....of what?
a better life? a rootedness?
Making a vital connection it is hard to live without
to be whole.

III

Before I was born he took the first step
in our estrangement
by changing his name from Feldman to Field
although even Feldman wasn't his name
(though he made Field mine).
In Europe it was Felscher
but at Immigration they wrote down Feldman.
And what's the difference,
wasn't that a good Jewish name?

As we came, he named us like lords and ladies:
Adele, Alice, Edward, Richard, Robert, and Barbara,
and moved as far from the lower east side as he could
to a town in the Anglo-Saxon protestant world,

the real America.
He did not have to cope much with that,
as we did every day.
He went to work in the city
where, with his new name,
he was able to go into advertising,
at that time practically closed to Jews.
He couldn't talk to those people, or us
without stammering, or yelling.

He did not want to know
we hated the house, the block, the village
where the people didn't want us—
after all, that was his achievement in life.
The family was his world and he wanted it to be ours
and not adopt the alien ways around us.

He avoided the relatives from the old country—
even our grandparents we hardly knew.
He felt superior to them all.
We ate on Yom Kippur, though he didn't,
having a stomach-ache every year,
and mixed milk with meat,
though he drew the line at Christmas trees.

It wasn't even that he was trying not to be Jewish
but it was his way of being modern.
He and my mother spoke Yiddish together
but we never learned more
than the words for "don't hit him" or "to bed."
We were left out of the secret world
of their real identity.

When we asked about our religion

he said we were atheists, and we shocked everybody
by going around insisting on it.
But when we asked him our nationality
he said we were American Jews
which in our town just meant Jews.
And what does God have to do with it?
You don't need God to be a Jew.
Anyway, we were beaten up
whether we believed in God or not
for a Jew was automatically an atheist to them.
Or maybe we were beaten up
because everyone knew in those days before Israel
it was our role in life to be.

Some people once met in our house
discussing whether to convert for the sake of the children
to save us from the Nazis,
for surely what was happening in Germany
was possible where we lived
with the Bund meeting in the high schools
and swastikas painted all over—
but we knew nothing could be done
to make you anything but a Jew.
Change your name to Field
and they call you Fieldinsky.

There was a kind of native fascism there
where the people disliked everything darker,
everything foreign, races that bred fast,
with daughters developing large breasts early,
races that did not understand conformity
but stuck to what they were.

Everything closer to New York was inferior,

even girls living the next town nearer.
Speaking a foreign language was unthinkable
and having foreign parents unbearable.

They didn't like me and with good reason:
my long, hooked nose; kinky, black hair;
wrinkly skin on the back of my hands —
I was a small, skinny, dark, and dirty boy,
my prick was button-sized and circumcised,
my parents spoke Yiddish
and I had lots of sisters and brothers.
We were animals.

My father ignored everything.
He didn't want us to be like the townsfolk
but to be an enclave, a ghetto, with him the master.
He made rules. Many things were forbidden:
    to believe in God, heaven, angels, or ghosts —
        all superstitions;
    to listen to jazz or popular music — for the goyim —
        or chamber music, or Wagner or Sibelius — Nazis;
    to participate in school activities or sports —
        for the goyim who were not serious about life;
    to care about your looks, clothes —
        tinsel, for the goyim;
    to mind being different and want to be popular —
        contemptible;
    and any evidence of sexuality was most forbidden —
        for bums.
In short, it was forbidden to have fun.
Duties around the house came first,
practicing music, and homework.

My parents made fun of everyone,

the neighbor who claimed to like opera,
the girl who wanted to be a movie star;
this one spent cultural evenings,
that one fell for the flattery of salesgirls and men;
above all anyone who was pleased with himself
or spent money on his pleasures;
and of course the goyim for their narrow, orderly lives.
All the relatives were torn to bits.

There's the main sin of Jewish parents,
being overcritical,
so you grow up ashamed of yourself, worthless
(if they don't love you you must be worthless),
more critical of yourself than anyone could ever be,
ridiculing what you long for, what you need to go on living,
ashamed to admit you want love, or anything,
and denying it to the end.
Even ashamed of being ashamed.

You dream only of running away.
My soul, but not my lips, cried out,
"Doesn't anyone want a little boy?"
But there was nobody out there
who would ever want someone like me,
who would ever take me in.

My father's theory of child-raising
was that it doesn't matter what you do to them, what
        they hear—
you feed them, clothe them, house them, and train them,
and they grow up adults,
that state of being grownup I could hardly wait for,
and by some magic all the terror and guilt
and self-loathing would go away.

Our sexuality would start to function
the way it was expected to,
and we would become famous.
Or more important,
we wouldn't do anything to shame him.

IV

Yiskidor, when he dies I won't know the Hebrew words to say.
Yiskidor, I won't be able to help the soul he doesn't believe
    in find rest.
Yiskidor, I go through life cut off from my ancestors.
Yiskidor, I live a life of shit.
Yiskidor, I'm a bum, I'm no man, I'm not even at the
    beginning.
Yiskidor, I don't know the prayers.
Yiskidor, I don't know the sacred rites.
Yiskidor, I buried my friend Alfred and it was done badly,
    nobody wailed, nobody tore their clothes—
    I didn't know you were supposed to,
    though somehow I felt like doing it.
Yiskidor, I took a clod of earth from the grave
    and have placed it in my shrine with his books
    and the letter from Jerusalem telling how he died
    of alcohol and drugs like a movie star,
    his dogs barking to alert the neighbors.
    He always reminded me of Marilyn Monroe—
    he had that ultimate glamour
    and went around in a cloud of admiration,
    though he never felt loved.
    Like a good Jew, he went to Jerusalem to die
    but his family brought him back

and buried him in Staten Island.
Yiskidor, when the clods hit the coffin I bawled
and everybody turned and stared at me.

Yiskidor, I pray for my mother every way I can
though I don't know the prayers to protect her.
Yiskidor, how she suffers, my mommeh.
I promised I would take her to California when I
grew up
and we'd live in a house overlooking the ocean,
just so she wouldn't suffer anymore.
Yiskidor, what is my sacred duty to my parents
but to honor them, both in life and in death,
for they produced me by the holy process,
Yiskidor, and if they fucked me up
they did not know what they were doing.

Yiskidor, and look what they gave me, the gifts,
my life's full of gifts, all my loves.
Yiskidor, for that little boy who didn't know it but was lucky,
with parents that made life hard,
Yiskidor, who complicated things for me
so I could never take the easy path
but had to choose my own
when all I wanted was to be standard:
straight hair, straight nose, straight.
Yiskidor, for that desperate wish I went to sleep with
every night,
"When I wake up I'll look right, be popular,
They'll like me."

Yiskidor, I woke up at last and they liked me
(even if I don't like myself)
so I don't read the "How To Be Popular" books

any more.
Now I read the "How To Be Saved" books.
They all say, Awaken,
follow the path of the heart
which leads to the east.
There is no one to blame any more
and what you become is up to you.

Yiskidor, and I believe them, I can't help it.
My family screams at me, Be skeptical.
I'd like to be but I can't.
Yiskidor, I see I had the perfect parents
for everything has turned out right
like a miracle.

Yiskidor, I had the illusion I could invent my Self,
I thought I could live by the rules of psychiatrists,
Yiskidor, I had the illusion I could get free of history,
not only our history, but my own history.
Yiskidor, but now I must go back to the beginning
if I can find it. It is surely somewhere
inside myself, still trapped
in that defeat at the first breath
when I understood my predicament —
which I chose.

Yiskidor, they have my love, the dear ones who are old now.
Yiskidor, all men and women are my brothers and sisters
now.
Yiskidor, how I love men, now that I have dared
to look in their eyes
and stand my ground as the energies connect.
Yiskidor, if men would reach out and hold each other
they would know we are all brothers.

Yiskidor, I am my father's son, God help me.
Yiskidor, I am my father's son, the heir
            to the mess he couldn't solve.
Yiskidor, thank God I am my mother's son too
            for what she gave me
            is what I survived by.
            I cry Mamma, and am healed.
Yiskidor, I am my father's son.
            Even if I can't stand it, still
            I am.

Looking Back

I can't believe where I am—
   on stage at the Guggenheim!
What did I ever do to deserve this?
It's such a pleasure being a poet,
   and a recognized one!

I didn't do anything, I swear.
It is as if the honor was granted
   just because I'm me—
the nicest thing to be rewarded for.

I don't even have to read my poems,
   just be here
     and you'll love me.
I feel so good tonight.
I'm going to take my time and enjoy
   every second on stage,
being looked at,
   looking back.

Bless you all for coming.

Sharks

Especially at evening
everyone knows the sharks come in
when the sun makes puddles of blood on the sea
and the shadows darken.

It is then, as night comes on
the sharks of deep water
approach the shore
and beware, beware, the late swimmer.